Muffin
Meals
& Memories

CHP Crystal Hope Publishing

Published by Crystal Hope Publishing

Book design copyright © 2015 by Rusty Hook Marketing & Design
Cover and interior design by Bryan McCoury and Jenna Miller
Photos by Julia Vradelis and Allison Worrell

Published in the United States of America

ISBN: 978-0-578-17429-7

A big thanks to Rusty Hook Marketing and Design for the fantastic layout!

About the Authors

Julia Eckert Vradelis lives on the North Carolina Coast with her husband and daughters. This is her second collaboration with her long time friend, Allison. Julia grew up in Mississippi and graduated from Delta State University with a BFA in Interior Design. In addition to turning recipes in to Muffin Meals, Julia loves to run, paint, play Bunco with her friends and travel. "Thank you to everyone who supported our first book and shared your stories with us. We feel truly blessed to have such a strong support group of friends, family, and our beloved 'Muffinheads'"!

Allison Arnoult Worrell lives on the coast of North Carolina with her husband and two daughters. She would like to thank them for their patience and understanding for allowing her to experiment on them with new Muffin Meals and traveling to promote the first book. Allison has had so much fun since Muffin Meals hit the shelves and is thankful for all of the people she has met that have shared their stories and their love of Hospice. She is a veterinarian and co owner of PetDocks Veterinary Hospital with her husband. She attended the University of Georgia and is still a loyal Bulldog! She loves boating on the Crystal Coast, gardening, playing Banjo, traveling to new places and catching some live music.

Dedication

Our first book, Muffin Meals, was dedicated to our beautiful Mothers, who both passed away from cancer. They inspired us in so many ways and have been with us in spirit throughout this entire process. A portion of the proceeds from this book will, again, be given to Hospice in their memory.

When it came to our "Dedication" for the second book, however, we were immediately in agreement that it would be all of you! From our first book signing, to our first retail store, our friends, family, rep groups, suppliers, publisher, and our devoted "Muffinheads" have kept us going and cheered us on the entire way! So thank you to everyone who has bought a book, our pans, our Haute Mitts, tried our recipes, shared some of theirs and supported us. We truly couldn't have done it without you!

People ask us quite often if we thought the book would be this well received. Trying not to seem "arrogant" we have to say, "YES"! Why do anything with the thought of failing? With that said, it hasn't always been easy. In the beginning, we were told "no", we made mistakes, and we had our doubts. But thanks to a wonderful support group, we marched on.   We have been all over doing book signings, sometimes for a big crowd, sometimes for 1 or 2 people. We have been on several morning shows, some good, some less than good. We've done a lot of trade shows, made a lot of sales calls, and simply worked hard to get this far with products we truly believe in. We are pleased to say that we are now in retail stores all over the country and growing every day, and we know how fortunate we are to have had all of you supporting us!

So thank you from the bottom of our hearts. We truly hope you enjoy this book. Please continue to give us your feedback (but only if it's positive and absolutely glowing about us) because we love hearing from you (again, only if it's positive and absolutely glowing). Make a Muffin Meal for someone you care about, and make your own memories!

Muffin On!
Julia and Allison

introduction

Muffin Meals and Memories is filled with recipes for delicious meals that you make in a Muffin Pan. As in our first book, you will find recipes for Breakfast, Lunch, Dinner, and Dessert. Most of the recipes are very simple, easy to freeze and are already in a perfect portion simply by being made in a muffin pan.

As we traveled around with our first book, Muffin Meals, we got to meet so many lovely people who shared their memories of some of their favorite meals with family and friends. So, Muffin Meals and Memories began!

Everyone has one – a family dinner or certain food that brings back fun memories (except for brussels sprouts. We can't imagine anyone having a fond memory there...but we digress) and we, with the help of some contributors, will share some with you. We hope many will bring back your own memories and put a smile on your face.

Food always brings people together, and we hope some of our recipes will be favorites of yours and your families' for many years to come.

Enjoy!

Table of Contents

Welcome

Muffin Meals are becoming a "thing". Regardless of whether this is your first attempt at making these, or you are already hooked (as we affectionately call our "Muffinheads"), you will enjoy the ease of making these recipes and sharing them with others. They are easy to make, perfect to freeze and reheat, and a great solution for busy people who don't have a lot of time to spend in the kitchen.

Mix and Match

After our first book, *Muffin Meals*, we actually learned from our readers some new ideas about how they use the recipes. As we said in the first book, with a little simple math, you can mix and match several recipes and cook them in the same pan. For instance, if three different recipes call for a pound of chicken, take the pound and make 3 different meals. Simply divide the rest of the recipe by thirds and you can make 2 of each!

Another great idea we got was to gather a group of friends or family on the weekend, make several trays of different recipes and then swap them so everyone gets one or two of each to freeze for the week. It's always more fun cooking with someone anyway, or make it a party! Just be sure to do any measuring before the wine starts flowing!

Portion-Control

We have been asked this question a lot – why don't you have a calorie count? The simple answer is that we are more about portion control than counting calories; however, doesn't one help the other? A huge hamburger typically will have more calories than a smaller hamburger. A 7 layer huge slice of cake will have more calories than a smaller cupcake.

Muffin Meals are made by you. You control the salt, fat, and whether you want to substitute brown rice for white rice, ground turkey for ground beef, and the amount you eat is controlled by the fact that these entire meals are made in a muffin pan. There is just so much you can fit in a large muffin cup no matter how hard you try.

The portion comparisons have been "keep your proteins to the size of a deck of cards, pasta to the size of a baseball, etc". So let's truly look at the size of a large muffin cup. Even if you wanted to, you couldn't stuff much more than a baseball and a deck of cards in to one muffin cup.

Obviously, we are not saying that if you make some of our yummy desserts and eat the entire tray, the weight will fall off of you- quite the contrary.   However, we believe, cooking in your muffin pan (or preferably OUR muffin pans) will make you more aware of what a portion size should be.

We actually had someone contact us, after she started using our first cookbook, who was mad at us.   "Now that I'm used to a normal portion size, I hate eating out anymore knowing how huge the portions are that they serve you in restaurants!" Our intent is certainly not to make you hate restaurants. You have to go out and have fun every once in a while but, hopefully, our cookbook will make you aware of how much you eat.

In addition to portion-control, our recipes offer an alternative to those "healthy" frozen dinners, most of which are pumped full of preservatives, high sodium, and other hidden "no no's". Muffin Meals freeze well and are a perfect alternative to fast food or store bought frozen dinners!

We don't begin to claim that we are dietitians, nutrition experts, or even great cooks. We are busy women, with busy families who have come up with a way to have "fast food" in a healthier way at home and control the portion so you don't have to think about it.

Eat less. Move more. It can be that simple.

Do you know the Muffin Pan?

If you have purchased this book and don't have any muffin pans, you are probably in a bit of trouble. If you have purchased this book and don't have Muffin Meals Muffin Pans then you're in a LOT of trouble. Just kidding. Sort of. (Available at muffinmeals.net or a retailer near you). Shameless advertisement...

Typically, our entrées are made in the Jumbo (large or Texas-style) muffin pan, our desserts and breakfast recipes are made in the regular size, and almost all of the recipes can be made in the mini muffin pans for smaller bites or appetizers.

Muffin Pulls

Muffin Pulls (patent pending) are our own ingenious way of pulling these Muffin Meals out of the pan. You can make them yourself by folding strips of aluminum foil or you can purchase some pre-cut in a heavier foil available on our website – www.muffinmeals.net. Either way, these will save you time and help protect our pans from you jamming a knife into them to try to remove the Muffin Meals from the pans.

Just crisscross in the bottom of the pan and follow the recipe. You can even wash these and reuse them.

With the exception of some of the recipes which have an actual crust, these are the only way to remove the meals and keep them intact. Trust us. We've made a lot of these!

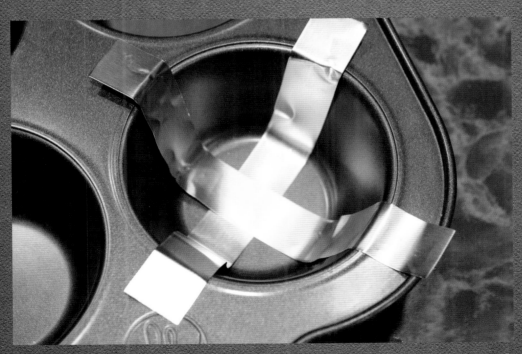

Beef Muffin Meals

"The only time to eat diet food is while you're waiting for the steak to cook."

— *Julia Child*

American Chop Suey
Memories

Family Influences

This is the ultimate Yankee family meal- Farmers, fisherman, shipbuilders, factory workers. A simple one pot meal (or in our case muffin pan!) that sent everyone to bed satiated and ready to face another grueling day at work.

My family is the epitome of the coastal Yankee (but we let his recipe in to our mostly Southern cookbook). Growing up, I found that everyone in the family made this dish. My Grandma, Aunt, Mother, Cousin... There were as many variations as there are people that make it! The basics were chopped meat, macaroni and tomatoes. Seasoning were usually plain, but it was not unusual to find Italian spices or even barbecue sauce.

I had many women in my life influence my cooking and baking. My Mom was the oldest daughter in a French Canadian family who were mill workers. Mom grew up as the family baker and caretaker when her parents were working different shifts. Being a military wife, she learned to cook a variety of cuisine as the family traveled.

My grandmother, my Dad's mother, Nana was born and raised in York Co, ME. Nana made everything from scratch and her specialty was fresh desserts with home whipped fresh cream right from the cow.

And finally, my grandmother, my Mom's mother, Memere, was born in Quebec and later moved to York Co, ME. Her family were dairy farmers in Canada and became woolen mitt workers when they moved to Maine. She also cooked from scratch and was quite the frugal cook as a result of coming from a large family. She was quite creative and cooked from her heart.

Brett took the influence of his Mom and Grandmothers, and with a longtime friend, Alex, opened his own bakery – Alex and Brett, in the coastal town of Morehead City, NC. Their bakery brought an upscale, international twist to an area where the only place to get a fresh cake was from a relative or neighbor. Brett has since moved back to be with his family, but Alex and Brett's Bakery is still thriving. We highly recommend a stop if you are ever in the area!

American Chop Suey

Recipe

Makes 6 Large Muffin Meals

Ingredients:

1 lb. ground beef, cooked and drained
1 can Italian diced tomatoes, drained
2 cups elbow pasta, cooked
1 tsp. garlic powder
1 tsp. salt
1 tsp. pepper

1-8 oz. bag of mozzarella, finely shredded
1 zucchini, shredded
½ cup spaghetti sauce
1 tsp. Italian Seasonings

Preheat oven to 350 degrees. Insert Muffin Pulls in Jumbo Muffin Meals Pan and spray with non-stick cooking spray. Mix together all of the above ingredients, or as Brett suggests, add whatever you have on hand! Fill muffin cups generously and bake for 15-20 minutes. Let these rest for a few minutes before lifting them out so they stay intact. Great hearty meal!

Beef Enchiladas
Memories

Beef Enchiladas are synonymous with my grandmother. Whenever she thinks I need help, she answers with wonderful food. Now that I have children, it usually comes in the form of cookies and pies. Back in the day, she would make the best enchiladas for me so that she could make sure we got a hot meal every once and a while.
But here is the memory...

We call her NoNo Nanny and I am finally going to tell you why. When my children were young and we visited her, her home was not child-proofed in the least. The result of having toddlers getting into everything was that she had to spend a lot of time saying, "No No". When the girls were old enough to refer to her with words, "NoNo Nanny" was coined and all the great grandchildren to come, followed suit.

-Allison

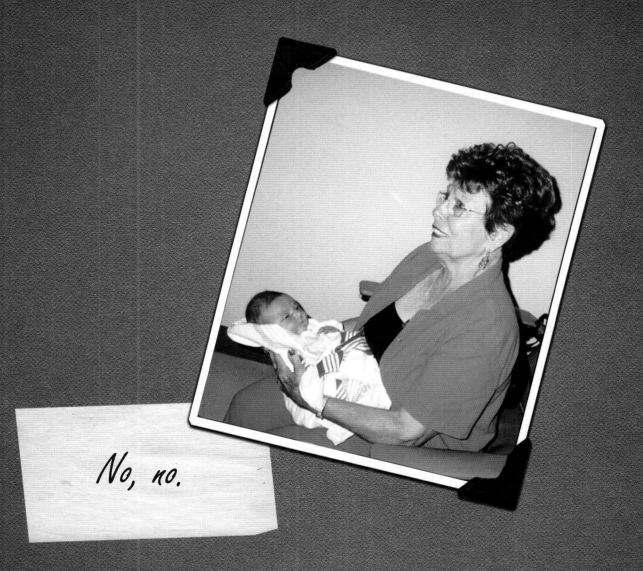

No, no.

Beef Enchiladas
Recipe
Makes 6 Large Muffin Meals

Ingredients:

1 lb. ground beef
28 oz. can of enchilada sauce
2 cups sharp shredded cheddar cheese
Large flour tortillas

Preheat oven to 350 degrees. Use Muffin Meals Jumbo 6-cup muffin pan. Place Muffin Pulls in the pan. Spray with non-stick cooking spray. Brown ground beef and drain. Add ½ can of enchilada sauce to the ground beef. Add 1 cup shredded cheese. Mix until simmering, then remove from the heat. Place approximately 4 Tbsp. of the meat mixture in a line down the center of each of the flour tortillas. Fold the tortilla over about 2 inches at each end of the meat, then fold sides in, overlapping. Then roll from the ends and turn on it's side. Place in the Muffin Meals Jumbo 6-cup pan. Drizzle each enchilada with enchilada sauce and top with shredded cheese.   Bake for 20-30 minutes or until the tortilla is golden brown and the cheese is bubbly. Serve with jalapeños, sour cream, or your favorite toppings.

Frito Chili Pie
Memories

Ok, immediately, this reminds me of my teenage years in the small town of Cleveland, MS. It was a beautiful town (and still is) but it was small. We had to get creative with our nights out. So we would go "ridin". My mother hated it when I told her we were going "ridin". "That's a ridiculous waste of gas," she would say, so, just like a defiant teenager, I just stopped telling her.

Those of you who went ridin' too will completely understand this, but for those who had better things to do, let me explain. We would all get in someone's car, (the DD for the night), and ride back and forth from Pasquale's Pizza to the Sonic. You pull in to Sonic, order your Frito Chili Pie and a coke or lemonade, and see and be seen. That's all there was to it. But I do have fond memories of it. Some of us veered off and went "parkin" but that's an entirely different event. And of course, I never engaged in such behavior.

Anyway, I asked some of my old high school friends to share one or their stories or memories about Frito Chili Pie or "ridin" and the response on Facebook got slightly off track. But it was entertaining so I decided to share the response rather than tell another story –

Julia: Ok my MS peeps…Frito Chili Pie will be making its debut in the next book. One of you HAS to have a story about "ridin" between Pasquale's Pizza and the Sonic to put in the book!

Paula: Can't wait for the story, sounds like a good one!

Lisa: Can it include Boone's Farm?

Julia: I think it has to Lisa!

Danny: I don't think we can publish the stories I have Haha!!

Jackie: Oh…my…gosh! I had totally forgotten about Pasquale's!!!

David: What kind of story do you want and how long?

Stephanie: My favorite! With pink lemonade!!

Tommy: Pink Lemonade with a little Bacardi Rum. If I had a penny for the miles I logged making that drive every Friday, Saturday nights and on Sunday afternoons. Told my parents once if they wanted to find me just park along that route and I would be by shortly. Lots of memories!

Stephanie: That's it! Bacardi! I couldn't remember what it was we mixed in the lemonade! Thanks Tommy!

Tommy: We made that ride a few times together, great memories.

Lisa: Pink lemonade and vodka for me! And some Reunite!

Lisa: None of which sounds good with Frito Chili Pie! Where were the margs???

Stephanie: Yum, margaritas do sound better, Lisa!

Julia: OK people can we focus on the task at hand? This is like herding cats!!

Stephanie: I'm sorry! Can you repeat the question?!!

Amy: I guess I was the only one that actually ate the Frito Chili Pies. Guess that's how I got to looking like this to begin with.

David: We didn't know what a Margarita was. Just the Red, White and Blue Budweisers!

Stephanie: Amy, I ate those all the time!

Danny: I couldn't afford a Frito Chili Pie – I was more of a pork rind guy…

Stephanie: I remember us cruising up and down the highway, stopping at Sonic for a Frito Chili Pie and Pink Lemonade so many times. I've made a few over the years trying to relive those days!

So…There you have it. Never got a story but memories were made.
Love these guys and I hope you all enjoy the recipe!

-Julia

Frito Chili Pie
Recipe
Makes 6 Large Muffin Meals

Ingredients:

1 lb. ground Beef, cooked and drained
2 Tbsp. chili powder
1 tsp. garlic Powder
1 can of Chili Beans (not drained)
1 tsp. salt
1 tsp. pepper

1 jalapeño, diced (optional)
1/2 bag of Fritos Corn Chips, slightly crushed or broken in to smaller pieces
1- 8 oz. package of shredded cheddar cheese

Preheat oven to 350 degrees. Place Muffin Pulls in Jumbo Muffin Meals Muffin Pan and spray with non-stick cooking spray. Combine all of the ingredients in a large bowl. Bake for 20 minutes. Remove from oven and let rest for 5-10 minutes. Now THIS is some comfort food!

To make this recipe healthier, don't make it. (We all have to splurge every once in a while, right?)

German Meatloaf
Memories

Mimi's German Meatloaf

My Mom made the best meatloaf. It's not up for discussion, it's just a fact. This is her second best meatloaf. (The original is in the first book.) She used to tell us stories of her big, tall, German Uncles sitting around playing cards and telling stories around the kitchen table. Food was always front and center and there was always plenty of rich dark beer.

Vera (or Mimi as her grandkids called her) never cooked a lot of traditional German food. However, once a month like clockwork, she would make spareribs, dumplings, and sauerkraut. Imagine growing up in a small Southern town and having a friend over after a day of sauerkraut permeating your entire house. Needless to say, I stopped having my friends over on those days. I actually liked it, but it was an acquired taste and it also wouldn't translate well as a Muffin Meal.

So, to represent my German heritage, I have chosen a more universally liked recipe. This is a yummy twist on the traditional meatloaf and should be enjoyed as my Great Uncles would have liked – with a side of potatoes, and a good hearty beer, followed by a card game. I'm afraid I have to insist or it won't be the same!

Wunderbar!

-Julia

My mom made the best
meatloaf. It's not up for
discussion, it's just a fact.

German Meatloaf
Recipe
Makes 6 Large Muffin Meals

Ingredients:

1 lb. ground beef
1 cup brown rice, cooked
½ cup diced onion
½ cup applesauce
1 tsp. parsley
2 strips of bacon, torn into small pieces

Topping:

1 cup of applesauce
3 Tbsp. spicy brown mustard

Preheat oven to 350 degrees. Insert large Muffin Pulls in to your Jumbo Muffin Meals Muffin Pan. Combine first 6 ingredients in a large bowl. Divide mixture evenly in muffin pan. Take your Muffin Meals Shell Shaper (large end) or the back of a spoon, and press the ground beef mixture to form a shell. Bake for 20-25 minutes or until ground beef is thoroughly cooked. While the "shells" are baking, combine applesauce and mustard for the topping.   Remove "shells" from oven and blot grease with a paper towel. Spoon on the topping and cook an additional 5 minutes.

Serve with some hearty vegetables and a nice dark beer and celebrate Oktoberfest whenever you like!

Green Bean Mashed Potato Casserole

Memories

I remember it being one of my favorites as a kid. For some reason, however, I didn't end up with the recipe until about a year ago. My mom mentioned she was making it for dinner one night, and I asked her for the recipe. I probably make it twice a month now as it is super easy and quick to make. Garrett and Alyssa both love it, especially Alyssa as she is a huge mashed potato fan. Maybe that's why I craved mashed potatoes when I was pregnant with her.

-Nancy, Newport, North Carolina

Recipes passed down three generations.

Green Bean Mashed Potato Casserole

Recipe

Makes 6 Large Muffin Meals

Ingredients:

1 lb. ground beef
1 small chopped onion
1 can French-style cut green beans
1 can tomato soup

Topping:

1 package instant mashed potatoes
(I like the buttery ones)
1 cup shredded cheddar cheese
Seasoning salt

Preheat oven to 350 degrees. Brown beef, remove grease, and add remaining ingredients. Prepare 4 servings of the instant mashed potatoes according to box directions. Place Muffin Pulls in Muffin Meals Jumbo muffin pan and spray with cooking spray. Put meat mixture in muffin tins. Top with mashed potatoes. Sprinkle Lawry's seasoned salt on potatoes. Bake at 350 degrees for 20 minutes. Top with cheese and bake 10 minutes more.

This recipe may be better than brownies!

Hamburger Cornbake

Memories

There is only one memory that I have about this recipe. It is the ultimate comfort food!

My mom was not a fancy cook but the things she did cook, she cooked well (and frequently I might add).

By definition, comfort food makes you feel good when you fill your belly.
Makes you smile perhaps. Well that is what I think of when I think of this dish.
Just like I feel when I see this picture of Mom and Dad.

Feeing good and smiling!

-Allison

Feeling good
and smiling!

Hamburger Cornbake

Recipe

Makes 6 Large Muffin Meals

Ingredients:

1 ½ lbs. ground beef
1 cup chopped onions
12 oz. can whole kernel corn, drained
1 can cream of chicken soup
1 can cream of mushroom soup
1 cup sour cream

¼ cup pimento
¾ tsp. salt
½ tsp. Accent
¼ tsp. pepper
1 bag of Egg Noodles

Topping:

1 cup soft bread crumbs
2 Tbsp. melted butter

Preheat oven to 350 degrees. Prepare 1 bag of egg noodles according to the package instructions. Then drain but do not rinse. In large skillet, cook 1 ½ lbs. ground beef and 1 cup chopped onions until brown. Stir in one 12 oz. can whole kernel corn (drained), one can cream of chicken soup, one can cream of mushroom soup, one cup sour cream, ¼ cup pimento, ¾ tsp. salt, ½ tsp. Accent, and ¼ tsp. pepper. Mix well and bring to a simmer. Stir in the cooked egg noodles. Place Muffin Pulls in the Muffin Meals Jumbo 6 cup muffin pan and spray with cooking spray. Fill each cup with the noodle mixture. Mix 1 cup soft breadcrumbs and 2 T. melted butter and sprinkle a little on the top of each muffin. Bake 350 degrees for 25-30 minutes or until noodles on top are golden baked. Allow to sit in the pan for 5 minutes before removing.

Hearty Beef & Potato Bake

Memories

This recipe reminds me of the most random memory in the entire book. When I was in school at the University of Georgia, I had a few favorite places to eat.

However, there was only one place for late night gatherings. There was something about a patty melt late in the evening that just topped off the night. For some reason, this recipe reminds me of "scattered", covered and smothered with a patty melt.

See you in Five Points.

-Allison

Oakland Ave.- Athens, GA

Hearty Beef and Potato Bake

Recipe

Makes 6 Large Muffin Meals

Ingredients:

1 ½ lbs. cubed beef
1 cup chopped fresh mushrooms
1 tsp. garlic powder
1 tsp. onion powder
¼ cup dry red wine

¼ cup beef broth
1 Tbsp. flour mixed with ¼ cup water
1- 20 oz. bag of shredded hash browns
Salt & Pepper

Preheat oven to 400 degrees. Brown beef in a large skillet with olive oil. (you may want to cut pieces smaller, depending on how large the cubes are to fit better in the muffin cup). Add next 5 ingredients and simmer for about 10-15 minutes. (You do not want your liquids to cook off so add a little more if necessary.) Add the flour mixture and slowly stir in to thicken sauce. Remove from heat. Insert Muffin Pulls in to large muffin cups and spray with non-stick cooking spray. Fill each cup ¾ full with shredded potatoes. Take your Muffin Meals Shell Shaper (or a large spoon or the back of an ice cream scoop) and press the potatoes in to the bottom and up the sides of the cup. Season potato cups with salt and pepper. Fill with Beef mixture. Cover the entire pan with aluminum foil and bake for 30 minutes. Let these "rest" for about 5-10 minutes before plating.

Serve with a nice salad and the rest of that red wine you opened! (Unless of course you drank it while preparing this yummy meal. I only say that because maybe it happened. To me. Maybe.)

Hot Tamale Muffin

Memories

This recipe will always remind me of my bridal shower/bachelorette weekend back in 1994. I got the recipe from one of my bridesmaids. My maid of honor had asked my friends attending that weekend to bring a couple of their favorite recipes written on recipe cards. We had a very fun weekend and this recipe always takes me back to that fun time with my dear friends!

-Nancy, Newport, North Carolina

This recipe will always remind me of my bridal shower/bachelorette weekend back in 1994.

Hot Tamale Muffin

Recipe

Makes 6 Large Muffin Meals

Part 1 Ingredients:

1 lb. ground beef
1 small onion, chopped
8 oz. tomato sauce
1 Tbsp. chili powder
1 tsp. salt
1/4 tsp. pepper
16 oz. can refried beans
4.5 oz. can of sliced black olives.
(Optional)

Part 2 ingredients:

1 bag of corn chips
2 cup shredded cheddar cheese

Preheat oven to 350 degrees. Brown beef, drain and mix with remaining part 1 ingredients together on the stove. Place Muffin Pulls in the Muffin Meals Jumbo Muffin Pan and spray muffin pans with cooking spray. Put half of meat mixture in muffin pans, layer crushed corn tortillas on top, add the rest of meat mixture and top with cheese. Bake at 350 degrees for 20-30 minutes or until cheese is bubbly. This may not be tamale by traditional definition but it is pretty tasty!

Hungarian Goulash

Recipe

Makes 6 Large Muffin Meals

This recipe is cheating a bit because it is actually made in a crock pot. The "Muffin Meal" part comes in to play with the bread baskets you serve it in.

Ingredients:

2 lbs. beef for stew, cut into small cubes
1 cup brown rice, cooked
¼ tsp. garlic
1 cup water
¾ cup ketchup
3 Tbsp. Worcestershire Sauce
¼ cup packed brown sugar

2 tsp. salt
2 tsp. paprika
1 tsp. dry mustard
Dash of cayenne pepper
¼ cup of cold water
2 Tbsp. Flour

Brown the beef cubes and season with garlic. Drain, and combine the next 10 ingredients in your crock pot for 4-5 hours on low. Combine cold water and flour until flour is dissolved, then slowly add to the beef mixture to thicken the sauce. Serve in your beautiful Bread Baskets. (See next page)

Bread Baskets
Recipe
Makes 6 Large Baskets

Ingredients:

2 cans refrigerated thin crust pizza dough
1 egg white

Preheat oven to 350 degrees. Turn over you
large Muffin Meals Muffin Pan and spray
with non-stick cooking spray. Roll out pizza
dough on a floured surface or parchment
paper. Cut out 12 circles to make the bottom
of the baskets. Use a cookie cutter or one of
your glasses that is the approximate size.

Cut the remaining dough into strips. For each cup you will need 12 2-inch strips and 3 strips 8 inches long. Take the smaller strips and arrange them around the dough circle pressing all 12 strips in to the dough to make them secure. They will stretch out a bit during the weaving but you can trim when you are done. Now place the other circle cut out and press. Take the longer strip and begin at the top (which is actually the bottom) and weave it over and under each of the smaller strips. Repeat the process with the other 2 strips but alternate the over/under.

Now simply trim this excess so it hits the pan and press together any "holes". Brush with egg whites to give the bread basket a shine. Bake for 10-15 minutes or until golden brown. These can be frozen to use later. Perfect bowl for Hungarian Goulash or any of your heartier soups and stews!

Roast Beef & Cheese
Recipe
Makes 6 Large Muffin Meals

Ingredients:

6 slices of whole wheat bread
1 ½ cups shredded cheddar cheese
1 onion sliced thin
6 thin slices of roast beef

1 tsp. sugar
½ tsp. salt
Creamy horseradish

Preheat oven to 375 degrees. Put 1 muffin pull in each cup and place the pan in the oven to heat up. In a saute pan, combine a small amount of oil, onions, salt and pepper. Cook until tender. Take the heated pan out of the oven and spray with non stick cooking spray. Immediately place a piece of bread (you will almost form a clover like shape) in each cup. Make sure you press the bottom down so it comes out flat. Add a small amount of horseradish in the bottom and sides of the bread. Add onions, 1 slice of roast beef, and about ¼ cup of shredded cheese to each cup. Bake for 10 minutes or until cheese is bubbly. Let these cool for about 2-3 minutes then pull out and serve with additional cheese or onions.

Here's what we did for you....we eliminated an unnecessary top piece of bread and we kept it in a nice portion size. By the way, if you are serving these for a casual supper night, we recommend having 2! It's still a very light but yummy dinner!

Saturday Noodle Bake

Memories

Spoons

In our extended family there were eight "Dads". We grew up spread out throughout the country which made our family reunions and gatherings that much more special. Since the majority of us were still up north, we would all get together when one of our Southern relatives came to visit. These gatherings were, of course, centered around lots of food, including the ever popular "hot dish" (or as the Southerners called them "casseroles").

The kids always had their own table, so we got reacquainted fast (even though it took us a while to get use to each other's "accents"). After dinner, the Mom's cleaned the kitchen, the Dad's smoked cigars or pipes and the kids played cards. The game most favored was "Spoons".

Now if you haven't heard of spoons, it is far too complicated to explain in a short story, (that's a joke) but it brought so much laughter to our group of cousins that it became a tradition every time we got together!

A couple of years ago, my uncle Sidney (Julia's uncle) died. We actually lost the remaining 3 brothers that year (one was my father, John). It was a hard time and we were blessed to travel to be with their family for the funeral. We were reunited with the bond of our cousins and yes, despite the sad circumstances, we played Spoons! We laughed, cried and taunted each other as we tricked each other into grabbing spoons at the wrong time. Of course, food was always around and we shared many memories as we played.

They say that cousins are your first "best" friends and I totally agree. The cousins in our family shared a bond. We didn't always see each other but when we did it was absolutely the best!

I'd like to dedicate this recipe for "Saturday Noodle Bake" to our Fathers and to our cousins who are no longer with us. Your memory warms our hearts. Thanks for the memories and laughs!

-Linda, St. Paul, MN

Saturday Noodle Bake
Recipe
Makes 6 Large Muffin Meals

Ingredients:

1 lb. ground beef, cooked and drained
2 cups cooked Egg Noodles (or No Yolks)
1 can of Tomato Soup
1-8oz. package of cream cheese cut in cubes

1 Tbsp. Worcestershire Sauce
1 tsp. salt
1 tsp. pepper
½ tsp. cayenne pepper

Preheat oven to 350 degrees. Insert Muffin Pulls in jumbo Muffin Meals Muffin Pan and spray with non-stick cooking spray. Combine all of the ingredients (try to combine the just cooked noodles so they will melt the cream cheese). Fill the muffin cups and bake for 10-12 minutes or until cooked through. Let rest for 5-10 minutes before removing. Great when paired with a salad and perfect for potluck dinners!

Memories

This muffin is a contribution from my lifetime friend, Diana, that grew up in USMC Base Housing while her dad was serving in the Marines. She lived in North Carolina at the time, which is ironic since many years later I live very close to where she lived as a child.

Also, this recipe is special because her family has always been like a second family to me. Her dad is no longer with us but I will never forget the times I shared with them at their home from high school to holidays. They always had a crowd gathering for food and fun. I still get to visit Ruby and she still makes me feel like it's a home away from home.

-Allison

1965

O'B and Ruby

SOS
Recipe

Makes 6 Large Muffin Meals

Ingredients:

1 jar dried beef
1 packet Country Style gravy
mix
1 loaf bread

Preheat the oven to 375 degrees. Place Muffin Pulls in the Muffin Meals jumbo muffin pan and spray with cooking spray. Shred the dried beef and simmer on the stove until warm. Prepare the gravy according to package instructions. Add the beef to the gravy and stir. Remove from heat. Cut approximately 10-12 slices of bread into cubes and divide in the 6 muffin cups. Gently press the bread in the muffin cup and up the sides. Fill each cup with equal amount of the beef and gravy mixture. Bake at 375 for 20-25 minutes until bread is golden brown toasted. Allow muffins to sit in the pan for 5 minutes before removing.

Poultry Muffin Meals

I always think if you have to cook once, it should feed you twice. If you're going to make a big chicken and vegetable soup for lunch on Monday, you stick it in the refrigerator and it's also for Wednesday's dinner.

– Curtis Stone

Buffalo Chicken Wing Muffins
Memories

This memory perhaps foreshadowed the events leading to you reading this book today.

As Julia and I have told the story over and over about how we became friends, this memory takes me back to the pre Muffin Meal days when I struggled to tackle a covered dish for a get together.

Julia frequently held social gatherings at her house for birthdays and holidays. One Halloween she planned a big trick-or-treat event for the kids with snacks and drinks for the parents. Since I love Halloween, I decided to appropriately bring something orange in honor of the theme. Cheese Doodles immediately came to mind but eventually I zoned in on a chicken and hot sauce dip that in order to make it orange, it was almost too hot to eat! At least it was memorable!

-Allison

Trick-or-Treat

2004

Buffalo Chicken Wing Muffins
Recipe

Makes 8 Regular Muffin Meals or 16 Mini Muffin Meals

Ingredients:

1 lb. package of chicken tenderloin strips
1 jar buffalo wing sauce
1 bottle blue cheese dressing

2-3 stalks celery (optional)
2 cups sharp cheddar cheese
1 can regular size biscuits

Spray Muffin Meals Muffin Pan of your choice with non-stick cooking spray. Preheat oven according to the instructions for the biscuits. Bring to a boil a large pot of water. Cut chicken into cubes. Place chicken in boiling water until cooked then drain and rinse. Place chicken in a mixing bowl. Next, add 1 cup blue cheese dressing, ½ cup of wing sauce, ¼ cup of diced celery (optional), 2 cups of cheese and mix. If using biscuits to make mini muffins, separate the layers in half and place half biscuit in a muffin cup. Place a spoonful of chicken stuffing in the center of the biscuit. Then press the edges together around the filling. Repeat with the other half of the biscuit, which makes another muffin. Repeat until all muffins are made. If making regular size muffins, place 1 biscuit in each muffin cup. Spoon 1 tablespoon of chicken mixture on the biscuit and press down until biscuit caves in. Pinch sides of the biscuit together surrounding the chicken filling. Bake according to the biscuit packaging or until golden brown. Top with more cheese, celery or blue cheese dressing for dipping if desired.

(Hint- the recipe will make extra filling so buy more biscuits so that you have enough to fill the muffin pan. You are going to definitely want extras!

Muffin on Muffinheads!

Chicken-n-Biscuits
Memories

The people you meet by chance are often the people that you create memories with that make you smile forever.....

When I was pregnant with my second child, I spent some time on bed rest and my mother stepped up as surrogate mommy to my three year old. She took her to preschool and dance class and fit right in with the other moms.

I remember her telling me about a fun and vivacious mom she met that was new to the area and couldn't wait for us to meet. When I got back into my routine, I met her. I still remember her introducing herself by saying, "I'm from LA...that's Lower Alabama!" Donna was such a great friend and a fantastic cook. I remember telling her she should open a restaurant and specialize in her famous chicken and dumplings and fried bacon!

She shared the recipe but I could never quite perfect it. When I make Chicken-N-Biscuits, I think of her and all the good times we had before she relocated with her family to Florida. Miss you Donna!

-Allison

Always Smiles

Chicken-n-Biscuits
Recipe

Makes 6 Large Muffin Meals

Ingredients:

3 cups cooked chicken, cut in small pieces
1- 8.5 oz can of peas and carrots, drained
1 can of Cream of Chicken Soup
2 Tbsp. sour cream

¼ cup milk
1 cup shredded cheddar cheese
½ tsp. salt
½ tsp. pepper
½ tsp. garlic powder
1 can jumbo flaky biscuits

Preheat oven to 350 degrees. In a large bowl, combine chicken and next 8 ingredients. Spray Jumbo Pan with non-stick cooking spray and insert one biscuit in each cup, pressing up the sides to form a cup shape. (You may want to flatten these in your hands before putting it in the cup – it makes it easier to work up the sides.) Fill each cup with the chicken mixture and bake for 12-15 min. or until the biscuits are golden brown. Top with additional cheese to serve. Sooo easy but soooo good!

Chicken Tetrazzini
Recipe

Makes 6 Large Muffin Meals

Ingredients:

4 cups cooked chicken
4 Tbsp. butter
¼ tsp. pepper
½ tsp. salt
½ cup chopped kale
1 cup chopped white mushrooms
1 cup reduced fat chicken broth

1 tsp. garlic powder
1 Tbsp. minced onions
1 Tbsp crushed red pepper
½ cup shredded mozzarella
½ cup heavy cream
8 oz. cooked linguine

Preheat oven to 350 degrees. Place Muffin Pulls in Jumbo Muffin Meals Muffin Pan and spray with non-stick cooking spray. Combine all of the ingredients in a large bowl. Place in muffin cups and bake for 20 minutes. Let rest for 5-10 minutes before removing from the pan.

Coconut Chicken
Memories

Mrs. Smith's (Grandma's) Pies

You won't get this connection, and shouldn't, but here goes....Coconut ANYTHING reminds me of my grandmother on my Mother's side. She lived in St. Paul, MN which was such a thrill for me since it was the "Big City". Her name was Vera Schroeder. She was always dressed beautifully with her pearls and such a pretty shade of gray hair. Every hour on the hour her grandfather clock would chime in the living room at the same time as her cuckoo clock chirped the time followed by the little German dancers. It was hard as a child to know which one should get my attention so usually we'd just run back and forth.

I don't recall my Grandma as being a fabulous cook (pretty sure my mediocrity in the kitchen was obtained by her) but I loved sitting down to dinner. It was always on her finest china laid out on a beautifully starched tablecloth. Even her apron was changed from her "cooking apron" to her fancy "only for show" apron.

All of dinner was a fabulous display, but my favorite thing was her desserts. Even though she slaved for hours over every little detail of the main course, dessert simply came out of a box. Mrs. Smith's frozen coconut pie was her dessert of choice more often than not. My mother never served anything store-bought so to me this made my Grandmother very "hip". I remember savoring that slice of frozen deliciousness with a cool breeze coming in the window, the sound of traffic on her street, and, of course, the clocks announcing the time.

Mrs. Smith's frozen coconut pie to a recipe for a coconut Chicken Muffin Meal may seem like a stretch but it's what came to mind. Isn't it funny what memories certain foods evoke?

By the way, I still have the Grandfather Clock and it works perfectly. The cuckoo clock is currently in storage but maybe, one day, when we have grandchildren...

-Julia

Her name was Vera Schroder

Coconut Chicken
Recipe

Makes 6 Large Muffin Meals

Ingredients:

4 cups cooked chicken, shredded
¼ cup chopped dry roasted peanuts
½ tsp. minced garlic
½ cup cream of coconut
2 cups Cooked brown rice
1 Tbsp. lemon juice
1 tsp. crushed red pepper

Preheat oven to 350 degrees. Place Muffin Pulls in Large Muffin Meals cups and spray with non-stick cooking spray. Combine all ingredients and put in muffin cups (almost "over-stuff" these as they will settle when cooking). Bake for 10-12 minutes. Let these rest for approximately 5 minutes before lifting from the muffin cups.

Top these with a lemon wedge, or fresh jalapeños slices for a little kick and pair with a fresh salad or vegetable. A frozen tropical drink should go without saying, but we'll say it.

Greek Chicken
Memories

Welcome to the Family

So I married a Greek man. On our first date I asked if he was Italian (I secretly always thought it would be cool to be part of a big Italian family), he said, "No, Greek." Needless to say, it worked out, which brings me to the story of my introduction to many of my soon to be Greek Aunts, Greek cousins, Greek friends in a Greek home at my first Bridal Shower. They chose a "kitchen shower" theme which either meant it made naturally good sense for any new wife, or that looking at this blonde, Methodist, southern girl that I could use all the help I could get. The latter was true. Still is.

My Big Greek Family

Anyway, I opened each gift which included a recipe and then the bake ware to go along with it. I got some beautiful cookbooks, pans, bake ware, linens, but still wasn't comfortable being the focus of attention.   Being in this situation is nerve-racking enough, but with the matriarch of the family, glaring at me from the back of the room, it was almost unbearable. So I get to her gift. I open it, ready to impress her with my complete excitement and enthusiasm no matter what it is. It was a recipe for Lemon Chiffon Cake and it was accompanied by a can of cream of tarter. Now, I'm from the south, and we can make a simple "Hey" mean "Oh my God, you look amazing and I've missed seeing you and we have to get together more often!!", but I'll be damned if I could make cream of tarter seem like anything more than a spice I'd never heard of. With the exception of that one awkward moment, the shower was absolutely lovely as were all the women I met that day.

I know, this would have been a better story if it were attached to the Lemon Chiffon Cake recipe, but I never made it. I do, however, still have that cream of tarter.

-Julia

Greek Chicken

Recipe

Makes 6 Large Muffin Meals

Ingredients:

2 cups cooked, chopped chicken
¼ cup chopped parsley
½ cup chopped kalamato olives (pitted, obviously)
1 Tbsp. lemon juice

2 cups cooked quinoa
½ cup chopped sun dried tomatoes in oil
½ tsp. salt
1 egg
¼ cup chopped green onion

Preheat oven to 350 degrees. Insert Muffin Pulls in Muffin Meals Jumbo cups and spray with non stick cooking spray. Combine all the ingredients and spoon into muffin pan. Press down slightly. Bake for 15 to 20 minutes. Let stand before taking these out for 5-10 minutes. Just enough time to take a sip of ouzo, break a plate and dance in a circle! (It's ok, I married a Greek man so don't take offense!)

Top these with extra lemon juice or lemon slices, feta, olives or tomato slices!

Inside-Out Poppyseed Chicken

Memories

Food is comforting

Believe it or not, I actually had never made Poppy Seed Chicken until one of my dear friends brought it to us when my brother passed away. As many of you already know, if you have our first book, (and by the way, if you don't, then you should get it, because you shouldn't read the sequel if you haven't read the first)
Anyways...

I lost my brother and his wife to brain tumors four years apart. It was such a devastating time for my family but I have many fond memories I'd like to share- this being one of my favorites and one of the last we shared –

Randy, my older brother, was popular in high school. He was class President, he played football, he was active in our youth group at church, but, let's face it, he also got in to his share of trouble. Harmless, but still, let's just say he "paved the way" for my other brother, Jeff and me.

But later in life, we grew closer and got together often with our families.

I think it's fairly common that we weren't that close in high school, more like don't make eye contact with me so people won't know your my geeky little sister. But later in life, we grew closer and got together often with our families. When Randy was near the end of his battle with cancer, we shared a moment reminiscing. Just the fact that he had such a clear memory was amazing to me since his short term memory was mostly gone from the brain tumor. We talked about high school and "skipping lunch". I drove the same escape vehicle as he …the blue Toyota Corolla. Apparently he never got caught. I, however, was in the principal's office many, many times, since he stood waiting for me as I pulled in on two wheels. When I shared this with Randy he asked where I had been parking. I told him, "Behind the band hall of course." He just shook his head and said, "Didn't I ever tell you to park next door and run through the bushes??"
Advice a bit late. But a good memory.

-Julia

Inside-Out Poppyseed Chicken
Recipe

Makes 6 Large Muffin Meals

Filling:

2 large chicken breasts
1 can of cream of chicken soup
½ cup of sour cream
½ cup shredded cheddar cheese (leave out an additional 6 Tbsp. to put in bottom of cups)
1 tsp. salt

Shells:

2 sleeves Ritz cracker crumbs (approx. 3 cups)
¼ cup melted butter
1 egg, beaten
1 Tbsp. Poppy Seeds

Boil Chicken until tender, then shred. Add soup, sour cream, cheddar cheese and salt.
In another bowl, mix all ingredients for the shells. The best way to crush the crackers is to do it while they are still in the sleeves then open it and pour in to bowl.
Preheat oven to 350 degrees. Insert Muffin Pulls in your jumbo muffin pans and spray with non-stick cooking spray. Scoop a ½ cup of cracker mixture in to each pan. Take a spoon and work the mixture up the sides – you do not need to leave any in the bottom.
After you have made the sides, place an entire Ritz cracker in the bottom (it should be touching the side mixture). Put a small spoonful of shredded cheddar cheese in the bottom (this will help "glue" it together) Now spoon in filling. Bake for 10-12 minutes or until bubbling. Let rest in the pan about 5 min. before removing.
Serve with a side salad or green vegetable or fresh fruit. Has anyone not had this brought to them at one time or another?? Now you can bring it "inside-out"!

King Ranch Casserole

Memories

King Ranch to the Rescue!

A month after the Hurricane Katrina devastation, Houston was targeted for another big hurricane- Rita. The city was in complete gridlock with people trying to evacuate and getting no where fast. Cars were stuck on the freeway for so long, they ran out of gas, people were walking around on the freeway, it was complete chaos. My parents were in their early '80s at the time. They called and said they were stuck on the freeway, in route to their relatives three hours away. They declined to share the information that they were evacuating. My Mom said "well I made them King Ranch Chicken". I told them to immediately exit and get to our house because they were not far from us. The hurricane was a false alarm for Houston; however, it was a few days of city shutdown which equals party in the neighborhood. We were happy to have my parents safe with us...and of course had her delicious King Ranch Chicken for days!

I am so grateful for Hospice in how they handled my Aunt and good friend's last days. They truly have a God-given gift and are the most special people. Happy to be part of this cookbook that gives back to such a worthy cause!

-Carla, Houston, TX

King Ranch Casserole
Recipe

Makes 6 Large Muffin Meals

Ingredients:

½ cup chopped green pepper
½ cup chopped onion
1 can of cream of mushroom soup
1 can of cream of chicken soup

1 can RoTel Original diced tomatoes & green chilies, drained
2 cups chopped cooked chicken
12 corn tortillas
2 cups shredded cheddar cheese

Preheat oven to 350 degrees. Place Muffin Pulls in the Muffin Meals Jumbo cups and spray with non-stick cooking spray. Combine the first 6 ingredients in a bowl. Tear a circle shape out of the tortillas and place as the bottom of the meal. (It does not have to be perfect, just good enough to form the base when you pull them out after baking). Tear the rest of the tortillas into small pieces and set aside. Add some of the chicken mixture, then layer with pieces of the tortillas and continue the process until the cup is full. Repeat in the other cups. Bake for 20 minutes or until bubbly. Let this rest for 5-10 minutes before pulling out of the cups.

Rosemary's Cranberries

Memories

In November of 1966 I was a new mother and Thanksgiving was coming. We had always gone to our parent's homes for holidays, but my little Nicole was too young to travel. I decided to make a turkey, my very first, for my husband, Tony, in our little apartment.

It was to be a special dinner. I would improve upon the obligatory cranberry sauce, since I was tired of the plain, canned, jellied cranberry log. Remember those? So I came up with my own version using fresh cranberries.
I thoroughly cleaned the oven in preparation for the inaugural roasting.
Because my baby was colicky, I had very little time to prepare on that day, so the prep was spread over a week.

By Thanksgiving morning everything was ready. The veggies were prepared, the special cranberries cooked and chilled and it was time for the turkey. It was stuffed and dressed, placed in the roasting pan and tucked into the oven early, for the 3 hour cooking time.

We had such a small kitchen that the table almost blocked the oven door. Still, it was set festively with candles, china, silver and Thanksgiving decor. I checked the bird at regular intervals but, because of the close quarters, never pulled it out. When I thought it was ready, I opened the oven to ease it out.

Well, in cleaning the oven the week before, I had apparently placed the rack back in upside down.
So, at my first tug, it tilted sharply, slid out, catapulting the turkey & pan across the kitchen, under the table and into the wall. The turkey flew out of the pan, which turned upside down, splashing all the hot juices over cabinets, curtains, counters and walls.
The 15 lb. bird then continued in the opposite trajectory until it plowed into another wall.

It was like an accident happening in slow motion.

Grease went everywhere, my screams woke the baby and Tony came running!

In the end, after some additional roasting, we did eat the turkey. The cranberries were delicious & became a sought-after favorite of many Thanksgivings to come.
There was plenty of cleaning to do afterward, but it was my most memorable Thanksgiving!

-Rosemary, Long Island, NY

Rosemary's Cranberries
Recipe

Ingredients:

2 packages fresh cranberries, rinsed (Buy more and freeze for other seasons)
1- 15oz. can of Mandarin oranges drained (reserve the juice)
2 cups orange juice (Combine the juice of the Mandarin oranges and the orange juice to make 2 cups)
2 cups sugar
2 tsp. cinnamon

1 tsp. nutmeg
¼ tsp. ground cloves
1 Tbsp. ground ginger
1 cup raisins
1/2 cup applesauce (optional)

In a large (4 ½ Qt.) saucepan put cranberries. Mix sugar and juice and pour over Cranberries. Bring to a boil & simmer for 10 Minutes. Mix cinnamon, nutmeg, cloves & ginger together. Add to berries while simmering. Adjust spices to taste. In the last 2 minutes of simmer, add raisins and Mandarin oranges. You don't want them mushy. Stir often and do not let it boil over! It only takes 10 minutes, so don't walk away or you'll have a big sticky mess. It's happened. Let mixture cool before refrigerating. Add applesauce, if used. Serve chilled or at room temperature. It can be made a few days before.

Muffin Meals Suggestion:

What to do with the days of leftover Thanksgiving fixings?? Make it in to a Muffin Meal! Simply take your leftover stuffing and fill your large muffin pan about ¾ of the way. (Remember your Muffin Pulls and non-stick cooking spray). Take your Muffin Shell Shaper (or use the back of a spoon or ice cream scoop) and press the stuffing along the bottom of the pan and along the sides to form a shell. Fill with leftover turkey, cover pan with foil to retain moisture and bake for 10-15 minutes. Top with Rosemary's Cranberries and no one with ever know it's the 4th time this week they've had this food!

Pork & Seafood
Muffin Meals

"The most remarkable thing about my mother is that for 30 years she served the family nothing but leftovers. The original meal has never been found."

- Calvin Trillin

Hawaiian Pizza
Recipe
Makes 6 Large Muffin Meals

Ingredients:

1 – 6 oz. pkg. of Canadian bacon slices
1 can of thin crust pizza dough
Canned or fresh pineapple, drained
1 pkg. of shredded cheddar cheese

Preheat oven to 375 degrees. Spray Jumbo Muffin Meals Muffin Pan with non-stick cooking spray. Spread Pizza dough on a floured surface or parchment paper and divide in to sixths (these will be rectangular or square shaped). Place each one in the muffin cups and press up the sides to make a cup.

Layer remaining ingredients and bake for 10-15 minutes or until dough is golden brown.

Obviously, you can make just about any pizza in this format, but we recently added the state of Hawaii to our list of retailers carrying our products, so Aloha friends in Hawaii. We'll come do a signing anytime!!

PoPo's Shrimp & Pork

Memories

This recipe was my sister-in-law's Mother's recipe. Did you follow that? She was Chinese and her mother (PoPo – Chinese word for Grandmother) was a wonderful cook.
I remember as a starving college student, I was invited to her house for Thanksgiving and she made traditional Chinese food and a complete Thanksgiving spread. It was so much great food!

My brother, who at the time was just dating Mona, was trying to make a good impression on everyone. He talked to one of her Aunts for a very long time. He had her smiling and nodding to every word he said. He was feeling pretty good about impressing her, until Mona went over and told him that her Aunt did not speak one word of English.

He got an "A" for effort!

-Julia

PoPo's Shrimp & Pork
Recipe

Makes 6 Large Muffin Meals

Ingredients:

½ lb. of shrimp, diced
1 cup rice, cooked
1 ½ lbs. ground pork
½ cup finely chopped green onions

½ tsp. salt
1 tsp. garlic powder
½ tsp. black pepper
1 Tbsp. sesame oil

Preheat oven to 350 degrees. Insert Muffin Pulls in to large muffin cups. Spray lightly with non-stick cooking spray. Mix all of the ingredients together. Press in to muffin cups and bake for 30 minutes. As always, let them sit for about 5 min. before removing. You can top with soy sauce and some fresh julienne veggies or even bean sprouts.

You can serve these with a green salad and ginger dressing, and fresh steamed broccoli. Yum!

Round Noodles

Memories

My kids were Chicken Nuggets kids. I wish we had written our book earlier because meals that are round truly do have some magic spell over kids but, alas, my kids were almost grown up when Muffin Meals was created.

My younger daughter, Sophie, did have one thing that wasn't even "chicken-related", that to this day is still her favorite. You may call them tortellini, but at our house they were "Round Noodles".

I tried, through the years to use different brands, cheaper Alfredo Sauces, etc., but Sophie catches it every time. "Mom, you forgot the peas" (I was out of them and didn't feel like going to the store), "Mom, the sauce tastes funny" (Cheaper brand) "Mom, what's up with these noodles?" (I thought I'd try the Spinach noodles for better nutrition??)

Anyway, it wasn't Chicken Nuggets so I made it and will always make it when she asks. Let's face it, if my kids request anything I'll make it. It makes me feel like I can actually cook!!

This is the Muffin Meals version and I hope you like it.

 And no, she still likes the original better!

-Julia

Round Noodles
Recipe
Makes 6 Large Muffin Meals

Ingredients:

6 cooked Lasagna noodles
1 jar Alfredo Sauce
6 thin slices of ham or prosciutto
2 cups of cooked peas

½ cup of diced red pepper
1 cup of shredded Mozzarella Cheese
Parmesan Cheese

Preheat oven to 350 degrees. Insert Muffin Pulls in your Jumbo size Muffin Meals Muffin Pan and spray with non-stick cooking spray. On a piece of parchment paper lay out one of the lasagna noodles. Layer with Alfredo sauce and next 5 ingredients. Don't over stuff! Carefully roll up the noodle and place in the muffin cup (ruffle side up). If it's not fat enough, let if open up slightly and fill with more ingredients. Repeat with the next 5 noodles. Bake for 10 minutes. Remove from oven and it sit for 5-10 minutes before lifting out of the pan.

You'll never eat traditional tortellini again!

(Ok you will, but it won't look as pretty!)

Salmon Patties with Creamy Dill Sauce

Recipe

Makes 6 Large Muffin Meals

Ingredients:

3 Salmon filets, flaked
2 large eggs, slightly beaten
1 cup of crushed croutons
¼ cup chopped green onion
½ cup chopped celery
1 Tbsp. minced garlic

1 tsp. salt
½ tsp. pepper
1 tsp. hot sauce
Tomato slices and shredded lettuce for garnish

Creamy Dill Sauce:

½ cup nonfat mayonnaise
2 T. lemon juice
1 tsp. dillweed
¼ tsp. hot sauce (more if you like it spicy!)
¼ tsp. pepper

Preheat oven to 375 degrees. Insert Muffin Pulls in Large Muffin Meals Muffin Pan. Spray with non stick cooking spray. Combine salmon and next 8 ingredients in a large bowl. Put even portions in the large muffin cups. Press down slightly to fill cups. Bake for 20-25 minutes.   While salmon is baking, mix all ingredients for the creamy dill sauce. After removing the salmon from the oven, let sit for 5 minutes. Remove from pan, top with dill sauce, a slice of tomato and shredded lettuce!

Memory

To be fair, this is a new recipe we tried so there isn't a deep story or memory behind it. However, I will have the memory of trying this with canned salmon, before using the fresh (or frozen) filets, forever embedded in my brain, my sense of smell, and my eyesight. Have you ever tried canned salmon? It's disgusting. I mean, I don't mean to offend any salmon canners; I'm sure it's the best they can do with what they're given. It smelled like cat food and you still had to reach in and get the skin out and, I think it was a vertebrae or something. I'm just saying if you're gonna can something, wouldn't it just be common courtesy to take that stuff out first? I presumed it would be like opening a can of tuna. It was not. Get the fresh. You have been warned.

-Julia

Salmon Patties

Recipe

Makes 12 Regular Muffin Meals

Ingredients:

1 sleeve Saltine crackers
1 can of salmon (remove any bones or scales)
2 eggs
¾ cup diced red onion
½ cup diced celery

1 Tbsp. parsley
¼ tsp. hot sauce
¼ tsp. Worcestershire sauce
½ cup mayonnaise

Preheat the oven to 350 degrees. Place Muffin Pulls in the Muffin Meals regular muffin pan and spray with cooking spray. Crush ½ of the sleeve of crackers in a mixing bowl. Add the remaining ingredients and mix together. Roll into approximately 3 inch balls and press lightly into the muffin cups. Place a small bit of butter or margarine on each salmon muffin. Bake for 30 minutes or until golden brown and crispy.

Memory

I wasn't going to include a memory for this one because it's nothing fancy. I remember helping my mom mix these up and frying them in a skillet until they were nice and crispy. My favorite part was adding the salmon. Now remember, I grew up to be a veterinarian. It wasn't until I read Julia's salmon memory that I felt I had to stand up for the canned salmon! It was like opening a box of Cracker Jacks to me. You never knew what you would find while cleaning the salmon. I thought it was pretty cool!

-Allison

Shrimp Pizza

Recipe

Makes 6 Large Muffin Meals

Ingredients:

Pizza crust dough in can
1 can diced tomatoes (fire-roasted are great)
Parmesan cheese
20-25 large frozen, peeled and cooked shrimp
Shredded or string mozzarella cheese
Oregano

Preheat oven to dough instructions. Use Jumbo 6-cup muffin pan. Place muffin pulls in pan. Spray with non-stick cooking spray. Sprinkle cutting board with flour. Roll out dough and sprinkle with oregano. Spread tomatoes over dough. Use pizza cutter to cut dough into 6 equal strips. Place 3-4 shrimp on each strip of dough. Roll from one end to the other, loosely. Turn on side and place in muffin pan. Top with cheese and sprinkle with Parmesan. Bake according to time for dough, 10-12 minutes or until golden brown.

Spicy Tuna and Sweet Potatoes
Recipe

Makes 4 Large Muffin Meals

Ingredients:

2 – 2" Tuna Steaks
1 large sweet potato
Cajun Seasoning
Olive Oil
Arugula

Marinade Tuna Steaks in olive oil and Cajun seasonings (you control the spice!) for at least 30 minutes. Preheat oven to 375 degrees. Insert Muffin Pulls in jumbo muffin pan (no need to spray with cooking spray especially if you have Muffin Meals non-stick Muffin Pans). Peel and thinly slice sweet potato. Cut tuna steaks in to 2 pieces and place in muffin cups. (These should be big enough to fill the muffin cup.) Top with layers of sweet potatoes, drizzle with olive oil and more Cajun seasoning. Bake for 15-20 minutes – figure 4 to 6 minutes per ½" thickness of your tuna steaks.

Let rest for 5 minutes, pull out and top with arugula.

So good and so good for you!

Vegetarian & Sides
Muffin Meals

"Thanksgiving dinners take eighteen hours to prepare. They are consumed in twelve minutes. Half-times take twelve minutes. This is not coincidence."

– Erma Bombeck

Butternut Squash

Recipe

Makes 6 Large Muffin Meals

(or 12 Regular Muffin Meals Side Dishes)

Ingredients:

3 cups butternut squash, cubed
2 cups quinoa, cooked according to package
1 Tbsp. Cajun seasoning

2 tsp. rosemary
1 tsp. salt
1 tsp. pepper
¼ cup butter, melted

Preheat oven to 350 degrees. Place Muffin Pulls in jumbo Muffin Meals Muffin Pans and spray with non-stick cooking spray. Combine all of the ingredients and place in muffin cups. Bake 25-30 minutes or until squash is tender. Let these rest for 5-10 minutes before removing.

This is a great hearty meal or can be a great side dish with pork chops or chicken!

Corn Pudding
Memories

This recipe has become a staple at all of our family gatherings. When my daughter Jordan was about two years old, we were having Easter Dinner at Mom and Dad's house and no one could get her to try any of the veggies. My mom always tried to make sure everyone had a favorite dish on the table especially at holidays. When she realized that Jordan would eat her corn pudding cornbread, she made it every time we got together. Confession...I still do!

-Allison

A phone in hand even back
then— J and mom

Corn Pudding
Recipe
Makes 6 Large Muffin Meals

Ingredients:

1 cup sour cream
1 can cream style corn
1 egg
1/2 tsp. salt
1 ½ package Jiffy Corn muffin mix
¾ stick margarine

Preheat oven to 350 degrees. Place Muffin Pulls in Muffin Meals regular muffin pans and spray with cooking spray. Melt margarine and mix together with sour cream, corn, egg, salt, and corn muffin mix. Pour into muffin cups and bake 30-40 minutes at 350 degrees until brown.

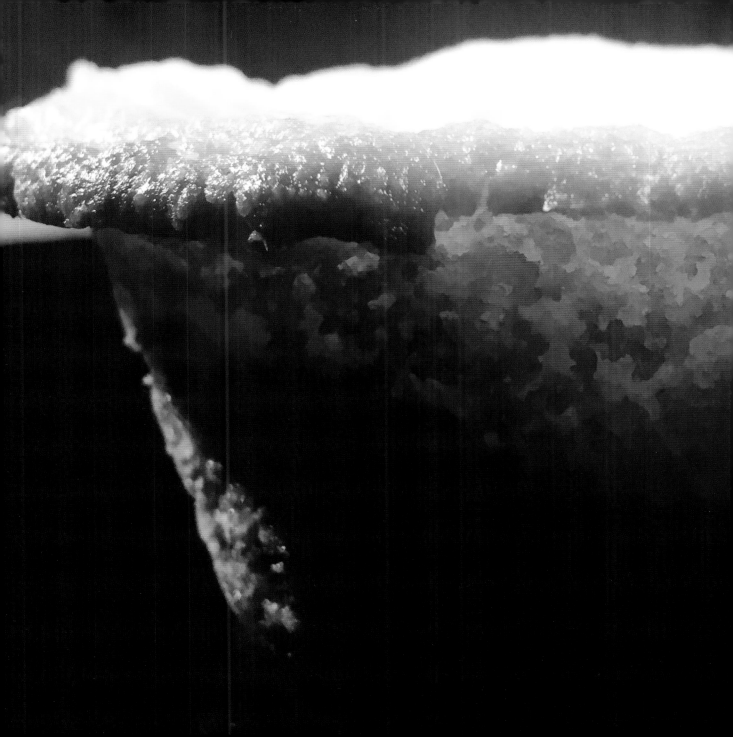

Eggplant Parmesean
Recipe

Makes 6 Large Muffin Meals

Ingredients:

3 small eggplants
2 egg whites
Italian Bread Crumbs + 1 tsp. garlic
1 jar of Spaghetti Sauce
3 cups of Shredded Mozzarella Cheese
½ cup of Parmesan Cheese
Salt & Pepper

Peel and thinly slice eggplant. Place in a bowl and toss with salt. Let sit for 30 minutes. Preheat Oven to 350 degrees. Insert Muffin Pulls in Large Muffin Cups and spray with non-stick cooking spray. Dip each eggplant slice in the egg whites then in the bread crumbs to coat. Place on a non-stick backing sheet and bake at 350 for 10 minutes. Remove from the oven and place 2-3 slices in the bottom of each muffin cup. Next layer with 2 T. spaghetti sauce, mozzarella and Parmesan cheese. Repeat these layers until the cups are full. Top with an extra layer of cheese and bake for 20-30 minutes or until eggplant is tender. Let these rest for about 5 minutes after you remove from the oven.

This is an easy and flavorful dish whether you're vegetarian or not!!

Pimento Mac-N-Cheese
Memories

My daughter, Hali, turned 21 when we were in Atlanta at the Buyer's Mart. Can you imagine having to celebrate your 21st birthday with your Mom (and your Mom's friend?) (No offense Allison)

I was thrilled, of course, to spend any time with my sweet girl and Hali was being a good sport despite her circumstances.

I won't go in to details, mainly because I don't remember them, but a good time was had by all. Hali got to sleep in the next day. Allison and I pasted on a smile and carried on at the Mart as best we could! Two days later we were still recovering and found a wonderful restaurant in Buckhead that served something similar to this dish. You know how good ole comfort food can just bring you back to life? It was delicious so I had to recreate it!

You can eat this anytime, but if you are nursing a hangover, I'll have to insist you make this. You're welcome!

-Julia

Pimento Mac-N-Cheese
Recipe
Makes 3 Large or 6 Regular Muffin Meals

Ingredients:

1 cup uncooked elbow macaroni
½ cup American cheese, shredded
1 cup cheddar cheese, shredded
1 cup light mayonnaise
1 – 2 oz. jar pimentos

¾ cup crushed croutons (We recommend Texas Toast seasoned croutons)

Preheat oven to 350 degrees. Place Muffin Pulls in muffin cups (If you make the large, it can be a meal, or if you use the regular size it becomes a great side dish!). Spray with non-stick cooking spray right before filling them. Cook the macaroni according to directions and drain. Combine remaining ingredients and fill the muffin cups. You will want to press down slightly. Bake for 15 minutes. Let sit for 5-10 minutes before removing! Now THIS is comfort food!!

Potato-Zucchini Rosettes
Recipe

Individual – Make as many or as few as you like

Ingredients:

Small Red Potatoes
Zucchini
Very thinly sliced Cheddar Cheese
Garlic Powder
Onion Powder
Salt & Pepper

Preheat oven to 375 degrees. Place muffin pulls in as many of the regular size muffin cups as you like and spray with non-stick cooking spray. This recipe can make one or 50! Start with slicing the zucchini lengthwise very thinly (I used a slicer for this). Each portion will take 4 thin slices of zucchini. Next wash but don't peel the potatoes. Cut off the very end and thinly slice the potato lengthwise to form the "petals". Lay out the zucchini strips in a microwavable dish and place potato petals at the top of the strip so that half is hanging over the top of the zucchini strip. Repeat on another strip. Sprinkle with garlic powder, onion powder, salt and pepper. (See photo 1)

Next put one thin layer of cheese the same width as the zucchini. This will serve as your "glue" to hold it together when you roll it up. (See Photo 2) Microwave just until cheese melts. Lay both strips slightly overlapping on your cutting board or another plate and top with 2 more strips of zucchini. Now you will have a longer roll width-wise. Gently but as tight as possible, start at one end and roll it up. (The potatoes edges should still be hanging out halfway). Immediately place in muffin cup.

Repeat this process to the desired amount. Drizzle with olive oil. Cover loosely with aluminum foil and bake for 20-25 minutes.

Here's where it get a little tricky. You want to let these rest for at least 5 minutes before removing. Then, remove but have another muffin pan available to place them in. If they sit in the original pan, the juices from the vegetables will not allow it to stick together. Leave them in the other pan for about 5-10 more minutes then remove and plate. (Another option would be to use toothpicks but just don't forget to take them out!!)

These seem more difficult than they are, and are so beautiful as a stand alone vegetarian meal or a lovely accompaniment to a steak or chicken breast.

And by the way, they're delicious!

Scalloped Potato Stacks

Memories

Where are the Potatoes, Toots?

My parents ate a lot of potatoes. I guess I never realized but they were at almost every dinner. This was brought to my attention early in my marriage. My husband said, "What's up with potatoes?" I tried to tell him that we did NOT have potatoes all the time and thought I would be able to prove my point the next time we ate with my parents. We all sat down. No potatoes. I had a smug look on my face as if to say, "See? I'm right. I'm always right. We do not eat potatoes all the time! Ha!" Just then, upon realizing there were no potatoes, my Dad said, "Hey Toots! (His name for my Mom). Where are the potatoes?"

-Julia

Ok. We ate a lot of potatoes.

Scalloped Potato Stacks

Recipe

You choose how many – one large potato makes about 4 Regular Muffin Side Dishes

Ingredients:

1 baking potato
1 onion
1 can of Cream of Mushroom Soup
Butter
Salt & Pepper

Preheat oven to 375 degrees. Place Muffin Pulls in muffin cups and spray with non-stick cooking spray. Peel and thinly slice the potato. Thinly slice the onion. In each muffin cup, start with a layer of potato slices, then onion, then a tablespoon of Cream of Mushroom Soup. Follow with more layers until it is almost overflowing (they will settle when the cook) Top with a dollop of butter and salt and pepper. Cover entire pan with aluminum foil and bake for 30-40 minutes or until potatoes are cooked. It is very important to let these rest in the muffin pan after you take them out of the oven. Then carefully lift them out and serve them up! If you didn't load them up and it looks a little flat, stack one on top of the other. These are the perfect side to a steak! Unless you're a vegetarian.

Shoepeg Corn

Memories

The Meltdown

Nobody hasn't at least witnessed a toddler pitching a fit. I remember before I was a Mother thinking, "why can't those parents control that brat?" Word of advice... never EVER say any of that stuff out loud because if you do, it will come back to bite you when you do have kids. It happened to me... during a Thanksgiving meal... and here's how it went...

I was visiting my brother and sister-in-law in Houston, TX. My daughter, Hali was with me and I was flying solo because my husband had to stay home to work. My brother and his wife had two children, an older son, Kevin, and their daughter, Caroline who was the same age as Hali (around 3). They had invited a few other guests who I did not know, prior to this, and they had brought their daughter as well. We let the kids go upstairs and play while we ate, as none of them were interested in a long dinner.

We were having a great time, sharing some great wine and food (this was the first time I had the Shoepeg Corn Casserole), when we heard a blood curdling scream. It didn't sound like Hali or Caroline, so the other Mom went upstairs to check. Then, the dreaded summons that no Mother likes to hear. "Julia, can you come upstairs? We have an issue." Apparently my precious angel, had stolen the other girls Barbie and wouldn't give it back. I tried that authoritative voice (that you use to impress other adults but rarely expect it to work on your own child) but Hali, apparently, really, REALLY wanted that particular Barbie.

I knew what was coming. I'd seen it before. I was going to have to peel it out of her tightly clenched fist and "release the beast". And so it began. For the next 30 minutes it was she and I going at it. I took her to the guest room to calm down where she screamed and cried and kicked me but I was not backing down. I was going to stand my ground. She finally gave in and calmed down and apologized to the other little girl, who had by now lost interest in the stupid Barbie.

I went back to the table, sweating, bruised and mortified, especially when I realized that the guest bedroom was directly over the dining room. Yeah, they all heard it. All of it. My brother just smiled and said, "Well that went well."

Ahhh. Toddlers..

-Julia

Shoepeg Corn

Recipe

Makes 6 Large Vegetarian Meals (or side dishes)

Ingredients:

1 can French style green beans, drained
2 cans Shoepeg Corn (regular corn is fine), drained
¼ cup diced green peppers
½ cup onion chopped
½ cup celery chopped

½ cup shredded cheddar cheese
1 can of Cream of Celery Soup
½ pt. sour cream
6 bell peppers (any color)

Topping: (Optional)

1 stack of Ritz crackers, crushed
½ stick of butter, melted

Preheat oven to 350 degrees. Cut off tops of peppers and seed (if you want to get creative, cut in a zig zag pattern). Rinse, dry and set in the Jumbo Muffin Cups*. Mix all of the main ingredients and spoon in to peppers. Bake for 20-25 minutes or until heated through. While the Corn Casseroles are cooking, combine the crackers and butter and add to the corn mixture as a topping. Bake an additional 5 minutes. Remove from pans and serve as a complete meal or as a side dish.

*If your peppers are too large for the pans, obviously you can bake on a cookie sheet using the same times. If you want to add a creative touch, soak corn husks (used for wrapping tamales} in water for about 1 hour. Place the husks in the Jumbo Cups (trimming to fit) then fill with corn mixture. Have your peppers cut and seeded and when you lift out the corn mixture using the husks as your "bowl". Just place the whole thing in to the peppers and serve.

Tomato Pie
Recipe
Makes 12 Regular Muffin Meals

Ingredients:

1 can pie crust roll
1/2 cup chopped yellow or red onion
2 cans of diced tomatoes, I prefer the fiery hot, squeezed to remove excess juice, roughly chopped, to yield approximately 3 cups chopped tomatoes
1/2 tsp. kosher salt
Oregano
2 cup grated cheese (combination of sharp cheddar and Monterey Jack, or Gruyere or Mozzarella, or Colby Jack)
1/2 cup mayonnaise
1 tsp. of Frank's Hot Sauce (or Tabasco)
Freshly ground black pepper

Preheat your oven to 350°F. Let pie crust become room temperature. Place Muffin Pulls in the Muffin Meals regular muffin pan and spray with cooking spray. Roll out the pie crust and cut in approximately 3 inch squares. Lightly salt the chopped tomatoes and set them in a colander over a bowl to drain while you are pre-baking the crust. Squeeze as much moisture as you can out of the chopped tomatoes, using paper towels, a clean dishtowel, or a potato ricer. Pre-bake the pie shell in the oven for about 8 to 10 minutes, or until lightly browned. Sprinkle a layer of chopped onion over the bottom of your pre-baked pie crust shell. Spread the drained chopped tomatoes over the onions. Sprinkle the oregano over the tomatoes. In a medium bowl, mix together the grated cheese, mayonnaise, Tabasco, a sprinkling of freshly ground black pepper. The mixture should be the consistency of a gooey snowball. Spread the cheese mixture over the tomatoes. Place in oven and bake until browned and bubbly, anywhere from 25 to 35 minutes.

Breakfast Muffin Meals

"I don't know what it is about food your mother makes for you, especially when it's something that anyone can make – pancakes, meat loaf, tuna salad – but it carries a certain taste of memory."

– Mitch Albom

Baked Cinnamon Pear

Recipe

Ingredients:

1 can crescent pastry roll
1 large can of pear halves
I to 2 Tbsp. margarine
1- 8 oz. block of cream cheese

2 Tbsp. light brown sugar
1/4 tsp. cinnamon
Vanilla ice cream, for topping

Preheat oven to 375 degrees. Place Muffin Pulls in each muffin cup and spray pan with cooking spray. Roll out pastry dough and cut into 12 squares with a pizza cutter. Place one square in each muffin cup. Place a small slice of cream cheese in each muffin cup. Cut each pear piece in half and place one in each muffin cup. Place a small piece (about 3/4 teaspoon) of butter on the top of each pear. Combine brown sugar and cinnamon in a small bowl, then sprinkle over the pear. Pull corners of the dough toward the center of the muffin cup. Bake for 8 to 12 minutes, or until golden.

Memory

This is a fruity spin on a recipe a friend suggested. She loves to share time in the kitchen with her nephew making new creations.
Quality time is the best!
Thanks Jenna!

-Allison

Breakfast Sushi
Recipe

(Makes individual Portions)

Best if done in the Regular Size Muffin Pan

Ingredients:

Bacon
Refrigerated Hash Browns
Shredded Cheddar Cheese

Veggies cut in thin strips (we used asparagus spears; however, peppers, onions, zucchini...would work!)
One small scrambled egg (uncooked)

Preheat oven to 350 degrees. Insert Muffin Pulls in regular size Muffin Meal Pan. On a cutting board, or parchment paper, lay out a strip of uncooked bacon. Layer with hash browns and cheddar cheese (don't go all the way to the end and, don't over-stuff!) In the center of the strip, place your strips of vegetables. Roll up carefully and place in muffin cup. (You will not need to spray with non-stick cooking spray – the bacon will provide enough grease!) Once you have placed the roll in the muffin pan, pour egg on top slowly so it will actually soak in to the roll. Bake for 20 minutes or until bacon is crispy! So easy to make one or a dozen!

Cheesy Potatoes
Memories

When I started at the University of South Carolina, I signed up for a potluck roommate match. I was placed in a room with a girl that would turn out to be a lifelong friend. Initially, it did not seem that we had much in common. We were from different parts of the country, had different fields of study and different groups of friends. Before very long, we were sharing stories, socializing together and planning a road trip to see her family. We headed off to surprise them and when we arrived her parents welcomed me as one of their own. Her parents made us the most fabulous potato pancakes and even though this is not their recipe, it is one of my roommate's and when I make it, I think of her family and that spontaneous trip! Love you Kathy!

-Allison

The 80's... the
fashion... the hair!

Cheesy Potatoes

Recipe

Makes 6 Large Muffin Meals

Ingredients:

32 oz. frozen hash browns thawed
1 can cheese soup
2 cup shredded cheddar cheese
1 pint sour cream
½ cup chopped onion
½ cup melted butter

Preheat oven to 350 degrees. Place Muffin Pulls in the Muffin Meals Jumbo muffin pan and spray with cooking spray. Mix above ingredients together. And place in the muffin cups.

Topping:

2 cups crushed corn flakes
1 cup melted butter

Mix corn flakes and butter. Spread/sprinkle over potato mixture in each cup. Bake at 350 degrees for 45 minutes or until topping is golden brown.

Crab Quiche
Recipe
Make 12 Regular Muffin Meals

Ingredients:

½ cup mayonnaise
2 Tbsp. flour
2 eggs, beaten
½ cup milk

1 can crab meat
½ lb. Swiss cheese
½ cup chopped green onion
1 can of rolled pie crust

Preheat oven to 350 degrees. Allow the pie crust to reach room temperature and roll it out. Sprinkle with flour if it sticks to the roller. Cut with pizza cutter into squares. (Approximately 3-4 inch squares) Place Muffin Pulls in the Muffin Meals regular muffin pan and spray with cooking spray. Place a square of crust in a muffin cup, and use a fork to press edges against the rim. Combine first 4 ingredients. Mix thoroughly. Stir in the crab meat, cheese, and onion. Pour into the muffin cups about ¾ full, and bake 35 minutes or until tops are golden brown. Allow to sit for 5 minutes before trying to remove from the pan.

Fruit & Granola Breakfast Parfaits

Recipe

Makes 12 Regular Muffin Meals

Granola Shell:

½ cup margarine or butter, softened
1 egg
¼ cup honey
1 cup oats
½ cup whole bran flakes cereal
½ cup chopped almonds
½ cup flaked coconut
½ tsp. cinnamon
½ tsp. salt

Fillings:

Vanilla Yogurt
Fresh fruit
Jam

Preheat oven to 350 degrees. Insert Muffin Pulls and spray each muffin cup with nonstick cooking spray. Mix first 3 ingredients. Add remaining ingredients. Divide evenly in muffin cups (about ½ full). Take your Muffin Meals "Shell Shaper" or a melon baller, and press evenly and up the sides of the cup to form a "shell". (If it sticks to the spoon, simply spray nonstick cooking spray on spoon). Bake 10-12 minutes. Let cool down before removing from pan. Fill each shell first with your favorite jam (we love raspberry or blueberry), then fill with vanilla yogurt. Top with fresh fruit!
These can also make great bite size treats by making them in your mini muffin tins. Great for brunch finger foods!

Monkey Bread
Memories

This memory is more about the name than the recipe. My mom helped care for both of my girls but when Lindsey came along, mom had her hands full!

Lindsey was always a little monkey.   From the time she first scaled the bars of her crib at about 18 months old, we had to keep the doors locked and the key out of reach so she wouldn't wander off.

One day when mom was at the house helping out, Lindsey went missing. We began to call for her and check the doors to make sure she hadn't figured out the locks.
After a frantic few minutes that seemed like forever, mom found her sitting on the top shelf of her closet giggling! She had figured out how to climb the wire shelving and was perched nine feet in the air hiding from us.

By the way, she was only about two years old!

-Allison

Making the most of me
A relative who influenced you
By: Lindsey Worrell

Have you ever had a relative in your life that completely changed your perspective on everything? Ever since I've known my grandma, I've looked up to her. My grandma was an amazing, hard-working lady. When I was just seven years old she passed away from lung cancer. Everyday she's been gone I've missed her incredibly, sometimes I think she's just going to come back, like she was just on vacation, I know it's not the truth. The truth is, God decided he needed another fantastic angel, and I guess my grandma was his pick. I know that everything happens for a reason, that's something my grandma taught me. Another life lesson she taught me was that whenever I was upset or having a bad day, that I needed to look on the bright side. When she was sick and could barley walk she never showed that she was dying. She always walked out of her bedroom, when I visited her, with her great big smile on, and that was what impacted me.

I've learned that if a sick little old lady can have a huge, happy smile every day that she is sick and close to passing away, I should never care about the little things that won't matter when I'm old and grey. Make sure to love and respect your family because they could be gone in the blink of an eye.

Poolside Lu and Nanny

Monkey Bread
Recipe

Makes 12 Large Muffins

Ingredients:

1 can of biscuit dough
½ cup of sugar
1 Tbsp. cinnamon
¾ stick of butter, melted
¼ cup brown sugar
Chopped pecans, optional

Preheat oven to 350 degrees. Place Muffin Pulls in each Regular Size Muffin Meals Muffin Pan and spray with non-stick cooking spray. Take the biscuit dough and cut into small pieces. In a large plastic storage bag, combine sugar, cinnamon, and brown sugar. Place several pieces of dough in the bag and shake to coat. Put the sugar covered pieces in your muffin cups and press down as you go. Add butter and pecans between layers. Bake for 20 minutes, or until dough is baked through.

Yum! But why is it called Monkey Bread? Anyone?

Sausage & Grits

Recipe

Makes 12 Regular Muffin Meals

Ingredients:

4 cups cooked grits (you may want to reduce the liquid so the grits are not soupy)
1 cup shredded cheddar cheese
2 cups cooked sausage (bacon can be substituted)
Salt & Pepper to Taste

Preheat Oven to 350 degrees. Place Muffin Pulls in regular Muffin Meals Muffin Cups and spray with non-stick cooking spray. In a large bowl combine all of the ingredients and divide evenly in muffin cups.
Bake for 10 minutes. Remove from oven and let these rest for at least 10 minutes.
Great when served with fresh fruit or eggs!

These also refrigerate/freese well and reheat!

Dessert Muffin Meals

"I always cook with wine. Sometimes I even add it to the food."

- W.C. Fields

Caramel Apple Spice Cake
Recipe

Makes 24 Regular Muffin Desserts

Ingredients:

1 box of spice cake mix and ingredients to make as directed
1/2 cup marshmallow fluff
1/2 cup cream cheese
1 can of apple pie filling (unsweetened)

Nutmeg
Caramel sauce
Chopped peanuts
Whipped topping
Apple chips for garnish

Spray non-stick cooking spray in regular size muffin pans. Bake spice cake according to directions. Let cool..Mix Cream Cheese and Marshmallow Fluff. Sprinkle with nutmeg. After muffins have cooled, remove from pans and cut in half. Spread Cream Cheese mixture on the inside top half and add a spoonful of Apple Pie Filling on the bottom half. Put top half back on. Pour heated Caramel Sauce on muffins. Top with whipped cream, nuts and nutmeg and an apple chip! Perfect for a fall dessert! (Since this makes so many, you can freeze the muffins and have dessert ready anytime!)

Cherry Tarts

Recipe

Makes 12 Regular Muffin Desserts

Ingredients:

2 ½ cups Graham Cracker crumbs
¾ cup melted butter
¼ cup of sugar
1 large box of vanilla pudding, prepared
1 can cherry pie filling
Whipped topping

Preheat oven to 350 degrees. Place Muffin Pulls in Regular Muffin Meals Muffin Pans and spray with non-stick cooking spray. Combine the graham cracker crumbs, butter and sugar. Place about ¼ cup in each regular size muffin cup. Press up the sides or use your Muffin Meals "Shell Shaper" to make the crust. Bake for 8-10 minutes then let cool completely. Do not remove from pan. After cooling, add pudding and top with cherry pie filling and refrigerate for an hour. To serve, just remove from pan and top with whipped topping!

Kahlua Mocha Cheesecake
Memories

The Meadows Girls

Cheesecake may be the ultimate dessert. Here is why!

You can never exhaust the recipe options for cheesecake flavors. If you could,
Cheesecake Factory would not have a two-hour wait to be seated just about any day of
the week.

When I think of cheesecake, I can't help but remember my old veterinary school
days and all of the wonderful times. The simple fact of experiencing such an intense
curriculum creates a bond with your classmates that is never forgotten.

One of my classmates was known for making the best cheesecake around. She had a
zillion flavor variations and I could not begin to select a favorite! Perhaps it was a hobby
that allowed her a stress release but we all benefited from some pretty fantastic desserts.

All these years later, she is still cooking. This time it's with her beautiful girls...and they
are cooking Muffin Meals! Thanks Ann!

-Allison

Kahlua Mocha Cheesecake

Makes 12 Regular Muffin Desserts

Ingredients:

1- 8 ½ oz. package of chocolate wafers, crushed*
5 Tbsp. melted butter
¼ cup ground pecans
2 Tbsp. sugar
1 Tbsp. instant coffee granules

2- 8 oz. packages cream cheese, softened
½ cup sugar
1 egg
3- 1 oz. squares semi-sweet chocolate, melted and cooled
1 Tbsp. instant coffee granules
2 Tbsp. Kahlua or any coffee flavored liqueur

Topping:

1 ½ cups sour cream
2 Tbsp. sugar
2 tsp. instant coffee granules

*For this recipe, we used the Oreo thin chip wafers. Another option would be the traditional Oreos but you don't want the cream in the middle. Someone will have to scrape it out and possibly eat it. Shouldn't be hard to find someone for that task!

Preheat oven to 350 degrees. Place Muffin Pulls in regular muffin cups and spray with non-stick cooking spray. Combine first 5 ingredients and spoon in to cups (filling about ½ full) Press in to the bottom and up the sides of the cup to form the shell. You can use your Muffin Meals "Shell Shaper", or the back of a spoon or even your fingers to do this. Beat the cream cheese at high speed until fluffy. Slowly add sugar, beating well. Add the egg and continue beating just until blended. Add the chocolate (make sure it has cooled a bit). Dissolve the coffee granules in the Kahlua and add to cream cheese mixture. Pour mixture in to "chocolate cups" (leaving about ¼ inch at the top for the topping) and bake for 15-20 minutes until cheesecake "sets". While it is baking, combine the sour cream and remaining ingredients. When the cheesecake is done, take them out and top with sour cream mixture. Increase the temperature of the oven to 450 degrees and bake an additional 3-4 minutes. Cool and chill in refrigerator for 12 hours. Top with chocolate leaves for a little extra panache!

Chocolate Leaves:

I have, in my day, made a lot of things out of chocolate. I'm working on an entire house. I'll keep you posted. Anyway, chocolate leaves are easy and add a little extra flair to desserts so give it a try. Just gather the appropriate size leaves from shrubbery around your yard (these should be straight from the bush, not off the ground). I use the back side of the leaf because there is more detail with the veins usually. Melt chocolate chips or you can use the melting candies found in craft stores. Spray or lightly butter the back side of the leaf and paint it with the chocolate. Immediately place in the refrigerator to harden. Then simply peel the leaf away from the chocolate!

Lumberjack Cake

Memories

Ahhh the Exchange Student....

Did you have an Exchange Student at your school? We did. Even in the small town of Cleveland, MS. We had several actually and they were always so "exotic" or at least it seemed that way to a small town such as ours. Anyone without a thick Southern accent AND from outside our little world was intriguing.

I remember we got an exchange student at the beginning of my senior year. She was from Durban, South Africa and had beautiful blonde hair, a glowing tan, and a wonderful accent. Naturally, we hated her. Mainly because all the guys loved her. But, it didn't take long to get to know her and we became life long friends.

Susan had such a fun spirit and, enjoyed our little town and her group of friends so much that she chose to stay in Cleveland for another semester of her freshman year of college. During that year and a half we had a lot of laughs, got in to a little trouble, and had a great time. We even taught her the fine art of " t.p.ing" someone's house, and which fast food restaurants benevolently donated toilet paper for the cause. (Usually they didn't know they made the donation, but still...)

At the end of her stay, a group of us went with her to the airport to say our "goodbyes" and even though I wished we'd see each other again, I thought it probably wouldn't happen. 20+ years later, she came back to visit and although I no longer lived in Cleveland, I made sure to be there. It was a great reunion with her and other friends and I am so thrilled she submitted this recipe for the book.

Thanks my South African friend!

-Julia

Lumberjack Cake
Recipe

Makes 24 Regular Muffin Desserts

Ingredients:

12 oz. pitted, chopped dates
2 cups powdered sugar
2 tsp. baking powder
1 cup butter
2 eggs
2 cups flour
2 tsp. vanilla extract
4 Granny Smith apples diced

Topping:

1 cup brown sugar
½ cup butter
¾ cup shredded coconut
1/3 cup milk

Combine dates with 2 cups hot water and baking soda and set aside for 1 hour. Place Muffin Pulls in regular size Muffin Meals Muffin Cups and Spray with non-stick cooking spray. Preheat oven to 350 degrees. Beat butter, sugar till light and fluffy. Add eggs, beat until combined. Sift flour and stir into mixture. Add vanilla. Mix in dates (in the liquid) and apples. Place in Muffin Cups and bake for 20 minutes.

Topping: Place all ingredients in saucepan and heat stirring until blended (Can be done in microwave for 2 minutes). Remove cakes from oven and gently spoon topping evenly over surface. Return cake to oven and cook further 10 minutes or until golden. Test with skewer. Better made 2 days before eating. Keeps well in fridge and is delicious served with whipped cream. Freezes well for lunch boxes.

Ok. This recipe had more than our typical ingredients and even included "sifting" (what??) but it is worth it! After we tasted it, we couldn't stop eating it. We did not stick to our "Portion Control" philosophy.

A big delicious cake that never fails to impress. The only downside is keeping it for a day to mature without tasting it!

Maple Butter Twists
Memories

Vera's Coffee Cakes

I loved the days my Mom, Vera, would make her signature coffee cake – Maple Butter Twists. I honestly didn't know they had a real name until I found the recipe after she had passed away. Everyone just knew them as "Vera's Coffee Cakes". She made them for church functions, bake sales, to take to a friend, new neighbors, or anyone that requested one.

But selfishly I knew that when she was making one for someone else, she would make an extra one for us. She would let them cool on a wire rack and when they were cooled and wrapped up, she would let me and my brothers get a spoon and scoop up all the maple filling that had oozed on to the counter. Yum. I mean...YUM!

Oh yeah, the coffee cakes were yummy too!

I had never tried making them before this, and I have to admit was very intimidated. But they're not as hard as they may seem and they are definitely worth it!

-Julia

My brother and I killing time waiting for mom's coffee cake to be ready.

Maple Butter Twists

Recipe

Makes 12 Regular Muffin Desserts

(Make sure you have 2 large pans for this one or you can adapt to make smaller twists in the regular pan. Adjust cooking time accordingly)

Dough:
1 pkg. yeast
¼ cup butter or margarine
2 Tbsp. sugar
1 ¼ tsp. salt
½ cup milk
2 eggs
3 ¼ cups flour

Filling:
¼ cup butter or margarine
½ cup brown sugar
¼ cup sugar
¼ cup maple syrup
2 Tbsp. flour
½ tsp. cinnamon
½ tsp. maple flavoring
½ cup chopped pecans

Icing:
(You may need to add more or less liquid to reach desired consistency. This needs to be able to drizzle)
¾ cup powdered sugar
2-3 Tbsp. milk
¼ tsp. vanilla

Soften 1 pkg. yeast in ¼ cup warm water. Combine butter, sugar, salt and milk. Stir in unbeaten eggs and dissolved yeast. Gradually add flour to form a stiff dough. Cover – let rise in a warm place 1-1 ½ hours. My mom always put hers on top of our fridge – but my fridge is built in so a friend told me to put it in the oven with the light on. That provides a warm place for the dough to rise! While the dough is almost done rising, cream together all the ingredients for the filling. On a floured surface, divide dough into 12 pieces. Roll out one portion to a 5 x 7 inch rectangle. (Continue to add flour if it gets sticky). Spread a thin layer of the filling over entire rectangle. Roll up starting with the 7" side. Cut roll in half lengthwise. Twist strips together, cut side up (you should be able to see the layers of filling on the top). Shape in to a ring and place in muffin cup. MAKE SURE YOU HAVE PLACED A MUFFIN PULL IN EACH CUP AND SPRAYED WITH NON-STICK COOKING SPRAY FIRST. Repeat with remaining dough. Cover and let rise in a warm place about 45 minutes. Bake at 350 degrees for 10-15 minutes or until dough is golden brown. Remove from pans and place on cooling rack covered with parchment paper. Drizzle immediately with icing.

Peachy Keen Kobbler

Memories

Peaches! Peaches! Peaches!

July 4 week was always an exciting time at the Davis house because it meant South Carolina peaches were on their way. Miss Nell (later to be known as Mimi) taught my husband, Barrett, and I how to peel, cut, and package peaches to put in the freezer. You may think it shouldn't require "teaching" but she had it down to an art form!

We would stand in the kitchen for hours to get them all put up. We had competitions to see who could keep the longest piece of peel intact and how many bags we could each get packaged. Naturally, Mimi always won! We had such a fun time laughing and telling stories, that it became something we looked forward to each year...not to mention the yummy peach ice cream and peach cobbler that was the end result!

20 years later, we still love to see those boxes of yummy peaches being delivered! Food truly brings people together!

-Beth, Morehead City, NC

Peachy Keen Kobbler

Recipe

Makes 12 Regular Muffin Desserts

Ingredients:

1 – 16 oz. package of frozen sliced peaches (or 2 cups fresh)
¼ cup brown sugar
¼ tsp. ground cinnamon
¼ tsp. nutmeg
1 tsp. fresh lemon juice
2 tsp. cornstarch

1 can of Honey Butter Flaky Biscuits (If you can find this kind you can use regular biscuits)

Vanilla Bean Ice Cream, and Praline Almonds (You can find these with the ice cream toppings)

Preheat oven to 350 degrees. Pour the peaches in a bowl and dice. (It's ok if they are still frozen. They thaw as you dice them.) Add remaining ingredients. Insert Muffin Pulls in your regular muffin pans and spray with non-stick cooking spray. Take each biscuit and separate them in to two. They will be too "bready" if you don't. (Yes, "bready" is a sophisticated cooking term.) Place in cups and form the biscuit dough up the edges to form a cup. Add your peach mixture and bake for 12-15 minutes or until biscuit is golden brown. Let these rest for about 5 minutes before lifting out.

Top with ice cream (use a melon baller so you don't overwhelm the dessert) and praline almonds.

S'mores Bites

Memories

The Fire Pit

You've heard of the "Money Pit" right? A term meaning you keep throwing money in to something that never seems to get better. This is how my husband may describe the year of the "CampWannaEataSmore" birthday party for our daughter.

I love to throw parties! And I love a good theme! If the two come together it's the perfect storm for me. It was my daughter, Sophie's 4th birthday and we decided on a "Camp Out" party. To be clear, there was never any intention to literally camp out. As you can see by the photo, that little girl was never going to camp outside with the bugs and heat. But we did create the illusion of going to camp, complete with Camp Counselors, Arts and Crafts, a Scavenger Hunt and a themed cake.

The name of our "camp" was CampWannaEataSmore so naturally s'mores would have to be a part of this in some way. Easy enough right? Yes, we could have just dug a hole and had a camp fire. In hindsight that probably would have been more authentic. But I envisioned a proper fire pit so against my husband's better judgment we built a fire pit.

I must say, it is a bit more involved than one might think. Between the big piece of equipment we had to rent to dig up the space, to the giant pieces of rock, this was becoming a bit more of an investment than just, let's see, buying balloons and paper plates.

When we finished, however, we were proud of our accomplishment, the party was a hit, and surely we would use it for many years to come. Come to find out, I don't really like the smell of campfire on my clothes and it never really seems to give out enough heat so...

There it sits, about 30 feet away from my back door, taunting me, and giving my husband this story to tell to anyone who will listen.
Still, "CampWannaEataSmore" is a fun memory.

-Julia

S'mores Bites
Recipe
Makes 12 Mini Muffin Desserts

Ingredients:

2 cups graham cracker crumbs
½ cup melted butter
1/8 cup sugar
Mini marshmallows
Milk chocolate chips

Preheat oven to 350 degrees. Place Muffin Pulls in mini Muffin Meals Muffin Pan and spray with non-stick cooking spray. Combine graham cracker crumbs, butter, and sugar. Fill each mini cup about half way with graham cracker mixture. Make into a shell by using your Muffin Meals Shell Shaper or by pressing with your fingers. Add a spoonful of chocolate chips and top with marshmallows. Bake for 10-12 minutes. If you want your marshmallows golden brown, broil for another minute.

Best s'more you'll ever have – without smelling like a campfire!

Stacey's Brownies

Memories

Calvin's Birthday Cake

When my son, Calvin was getting ready to turn 18, I wanted to make him a birthday cake, as I always have. He wanted something other than a traditional cake. Alas, the chocolate cream cheese brownies came to become a birthday tradition, and a Christmas tradition, and a Valentine's tradition...or just because!

-Stacey

We have to add a personal note to this one. Our
friend Stacey is not only a fabulous baker, a wonderful
Mother, and a "Rock Star" to her preschoolers, she
is also a warrior. Stacey was diagnosed with Stage IV
colon cancer several years ago. She continues to fight,
stay positive and is an inspiration to so many. When you
make these brownies say a little prayer for Stacey and
so many others battling the demon cancer!

Stacey's Brownies
Recipe

Makes 12 Regular Muffin Desserts

Ingredients:

10 Tbsp. butter
3 oz. Hershey's Milk Chocolate Chips
1 cup of Sugar
2 eggs
2 tsp. vanilla
¾ cup flour
¼ tsp. salt
2 Tbsp. Unsweetened Hershey's Cocoa Powder

Cream Cheese Swirl:

8 oz. cream cheese, softened
1/3 cup sugar
1 egg
Pinch of salt
2 tsp. vanilla
Hershey Bars to top

Preheat oven to 350 degrees. Place Muffin Pulls in Regular Muffin Meals Muffin Pans and spray with non-stick cooking spray. In a small saucepan, over medium heat, or in the microwave, melt chocolate and butter until smooth. Allow to cool slightly. In a separate bowl, beat eggs and vanilla with the sugar. Slowly add in chocolate mixture until well combined. In another small bowl, sift together cocoa, salt and flour. Add mixture to rest of the batter. Do not over-mix. Pour batter into muffin cups. To make the cream cheese swirl, beat ingredients together until smooth. Pour brownie batter in each cup. Take a knife and swirl the cream cheese into the brownie batter. Be careful not to scrape the pan. (Particularly if it's one of our pretty pans!) Bake 20-25 minutes or until toothpick comes out clean when inserted. Remove from pan and let cool slightly. Top with a piece of a Hershey bar.

Yummy!

Tropical Bananas Foster
Recipe
Makes 12 Regular Muffin Desserts

Ingredients:

1 ½ cups angel food cake cubes
1 Tbsp. butter
2 Tbsp. dark brown sugar
2 cups pineapple juice
3 Tbsp. dark rum

1 tsp. vanilla extract
¼ tsp. ground cinnamon
2 bananas, sliced
Chopped macadamia nuts
Whipped topping

Preheat oven to 350 degrees. Insert Muffin Pulls in regular size Muffin Meals Muffin Pans and spray with non-stick cooking spray. Spread Angel Food cake cubes on a tray and bake at 350 degrees for 5 minutes to toast lightly. Mix remaining 7 ingredients in a saucepan and heat on low until butter is melted. Next, take cake cubes and spread a layer in each muffin cup. Top with banana mixture, then repeat layers until filled. Bake for 5-10 minutes. Let these rest for 5 minutes, pull out and top with whipped topping and chopped macadamia nuts.

White Chocolate Fruit Baskets

Recipe

Makes 6 Regular Muffin Dessert Baskets

Ingredients:

10 Squares of White Chocolate (Or Dark Chocolate)
Fresh Fruit

Place Muffin Pulls in regular muffin cups. Place the muffin pan in the freezer. While the pan is getting cold, melt the chocolate and spoon in to pastry bag (with a small tip) or in a zip lock bag with a tiny hole snipped out of the end with scissors. Take your pan out of the freezer and quickly spray with non-stick cooking spray. You are going to make these baskets in stages, working quickly so the pan stays cold. First, drizzle the chocolate in the bottom of each cup. Be generous with the bottom part so it will hold the rest together. Place the pan back in the freezer for 10 minutes. Take the pan out again, and tilt it to drizzle one side of each cup and place back in the freezer for 5-10 minutes. Take the pan out and tilt it to do the other side. You can make these as "lacy" as you want or more filled in. You can even finish it with a pretty drizzle along the top edges. Freeze or refrigerate for 30 minutes. Remove from pan, fill with fresh fruit and serve!

Leave in the refrigerator until ready to serve.

These are so pretty and easy once you get the hang of it! Get creative and try to layers of chocolate – one white chocolate and then dark chocolate.

Perfect for showers or brunches!

Copyright Acknowledgments

No Yolks

Ritz

Worcestershire

RoTel

Lawry's Seasonings

Accent

Frito

Hershey